TANGRAMS

TANGRAMS

Picture-Making Puzzle Game

by Peter Van Note

CHARLES E. TUTTLE COMPANY
Rutland, Vermont & Tokyo, Japan

Representatives
Continental Europe: BOXERBOOKS, INC., Zurich
British Isles: PRENTICE-HALL INTERNATIONAL, INC., London
Australasia: PAUL FLESCH & CO., PTY. LTD., Melbourne
Canada: M. G. HURTIG LTD., Edmonton

Published by the Charles E. Tuttle Company, Inc.
of Rutland, Vermont & Tokyo, Japan
with editorial offices at
Suido 1-chome, 2-6, Bunkyo-ku, Tokyo, Japan

Copyright in Japan, 1966 by Charles E. Tuttle Co., Inc.

International Standard Book No. 0-8048-0567-9

First printing, 1966
Second printing, 1973

0276-000337-4615
PRINTED IN JAPAN

Table of Contents

How Tan Invented a New Game

A VERY long time ago in China—so the story goes—a man named Tan dropped a square tile on the floor. It broke into seven pieces.

Tan tried to put the pieces together again. But instead of a square, the pieces fitted together in the shapes of birds, sailboats, houses, animals, people—almost anything. Tan had so much fun making patterns with his seven pieces that he soon forgot why he had wanted a square tile in the first place.

When Tan showed his friends his seven-piece puzzle, they were delighted. They made seven-piece sets of their own from cardboard and made patterns for other people. Soon, people the world over were making Tangrams (which means, "Tan's pictures"), including such notables as Lewis Carroll, Napoleon, John Quincy Adams, and Edgar Allan Poe. And Tangrams remain popular to this day.

Playing Tangrams is loads of fun. Try it and see. All you need is a set of seven pieces (provided in envelope inside rear cover), which you fit together to make the Tangram patterns in this book. Remember: you need ALL seven pieces to make each pattern—no more, no less.

Here are some tips for added fun: (1) Have Tangram races with your friends, to see who can solve a pattern first. (2) Make Tangram pictures, suitable for framing, by pasting scenes of patterns on colored paper. These make unusual gifts. (3) And try inventing new Trangram patterns of your own. When you do, trace the pattern's outline on paper, and let your family and friends share the fun of solving it.

Many of the patterns in this book were devised by the Englishman, Henry E. Dudeney, a 19th-century fan of Sherlock Holmes. Others are by Martin Gardner (whose column, "Mathematical Games," appears monthly in the *Scientific American*), Sam Loyd, and F. G. Hartswick. While some are of my own invention, my personal favorites are from an ancient Chinese manuscript —possibly the inventions of Tan, himself.

Peter Van Note

New York City

Making Tangram Sets

You may want to make additional sets so that several people can play at the same time. Place a piece of good-quality typing paper over the drawings below and trace; then cut out the figures. These sets will fit the Tangram patterns in this book. You will find that several sets of Tangrams are necessary to complete some scenes or pictures.

When using other materials such as cardboard or colored construction paper, draw your set directly on the material to be used. A simple method of drawing accurate figures is given on page 7.

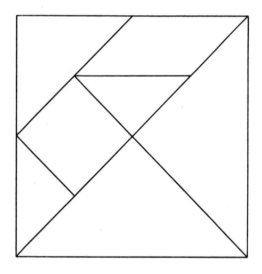

How to Draw Your Tangram Sets

1. Make a square of any size.
2. Bisect OB and OA; join CD.
3. Place ruler diagonally along OF and join EF.
4. Draw diagonal line AB.
5. Quarter AB; join EG and CH.

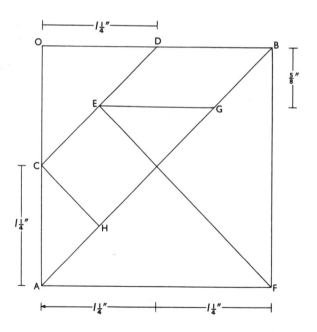

PART ONE
TANGRAM PATTERNS

THE HOUSE THAT JACK BUILT
(A Tale with Tangrams)

This is the cock that crowed in the morn...

...that woke the priest,
all shaven and shorn...

...that married the man,
all tattered and torn...

...that kissed the maiden, all forlorn...

...that milked the cow with the crumpled horn...

Pattern size: ¾"

Solution on page 34

10

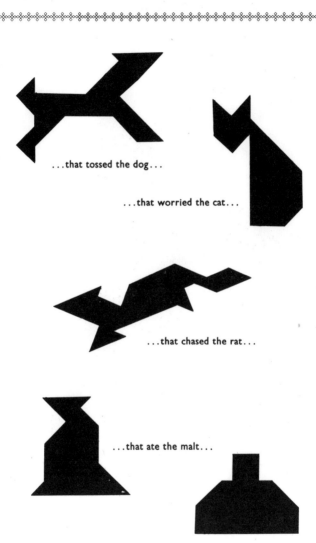

...that tossed the dog...

...that worried the cat...

...that chased the rat...

...that ate the malt...

...that lay in the HOUSE THAT JACK BUILT!

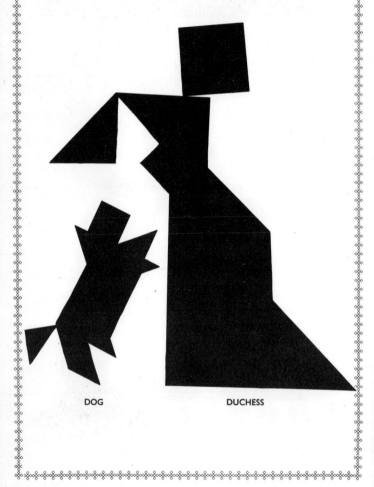

DOG   DUCHESS

Pattern sizes: 2"; 1"   *Solution on page 36*

MOUNTAINS

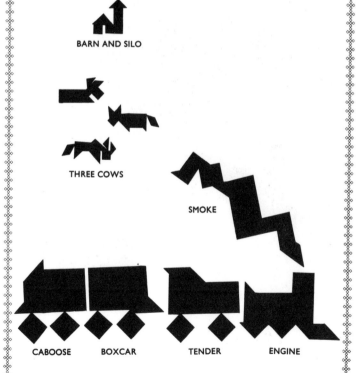

BARN AND SILO

THREE COWS

SMOKE

CABOOSE   BOXCAR   TENDER   ENGINE

Pattern sizes: $1\frac{1}{8}''$; $\frac{5}{8}''$; $\frac{1}{4}''$

Solution on page 37

13

ESKIMO WHALE HUNT

ICEBERG

WHALE

SMALL ESKIMO IN LARGE KAYAK

TWO ESKIMOS IN KAYAK

LARGE ESKIMO IN SMALL KAYAK

Pattern sizes: $1\frac{1}{2}$"; $\frac{3}{4}$"

Solution on page 38

14

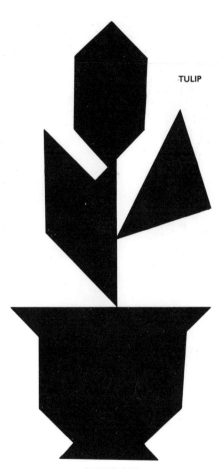

TULIP

FLOWER POT

Pattern size: $1\frac{1}{2}$"

Solution on page 39

THE VILLAGE BLACKSMITH

Solution on page 40

BLACKSMITH

FORGE

ANVIL

HAMMER

Pattern sizes: $1\frac{1}{4}"$; $\frac{5}{8}"$

Solution on page 40

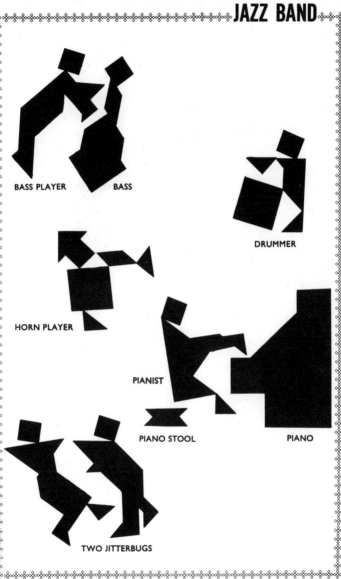

BASS PLAYER BASS

DRUMMER

HORN PLAYER

PIANIST

PIANO STOOL PIANO

TWO JITTERBUGS

Pattern sizes: 1"; ⅝"; ¼" *Solution on page 41*

TWO INDIANS ON HORSEBACK

SQUAW WITH BASKET

CHIEF

GOLDBRICKING BRAVE

Pattern sizes: $1\frac{1}{4}''$; $\frac{5}{8}''$; $\frac{1}{4}''$

Solution on page 42

MOTHER CAT AND KITTENS

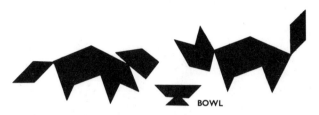

BOWL

TWO KITTENS AT LUNCH

THREE KITTENS AT PLAY

MOTHER CAT

Pattern sizes: $1\frac{1}{4}''$; $\frac{5}{8}''$; $\frac{1}{4}''$

Solution on page 43

CHESS GAME

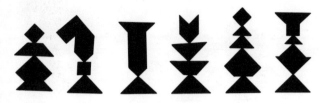

SIX CHESS MEN

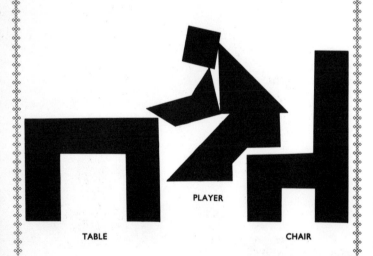

PLAYER

TABLE

CHAIR

Pattern sizes: 1"; ⅜"

Solution on page 44

20

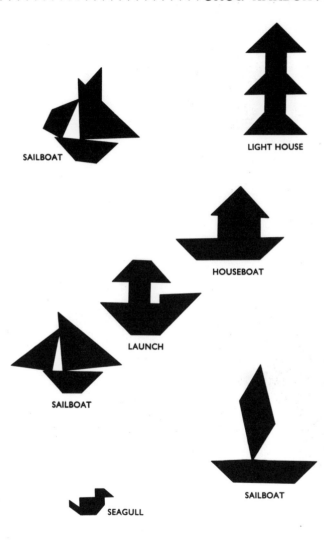

SAILBOAT

LIGHT HOUSE

HOUSEBOAT

LAUNCH

SAILBOAT

SAILBOAT

SEAGULL

Pattern sizes: $\frac{5}{8}''$; $\frac{1}{4}''$

Solution on page 45

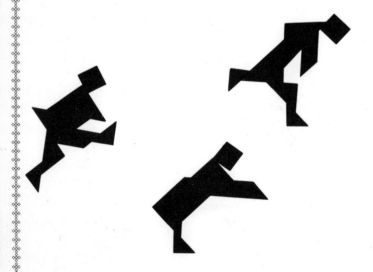

Pattern size: $\frac{5}{8}''$ Solution on page 46

POLITICIAN

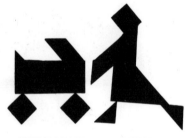

BABY CARRIAGE   NURSE

Pattern size: $\frac{5}{8}''$

Solution on page 48

EGYPTIAN SCENE

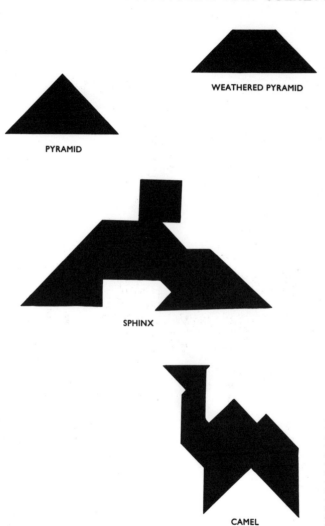

WEATHERED PYRAMID

PYRAMID

SPHINX

CAMEL

Pattern sizes: $1\frac{1}{4}''$; $1''$; $\frac{5}{8}''$

Solution on page 49

GOOSE

ROOSTER

GANDER

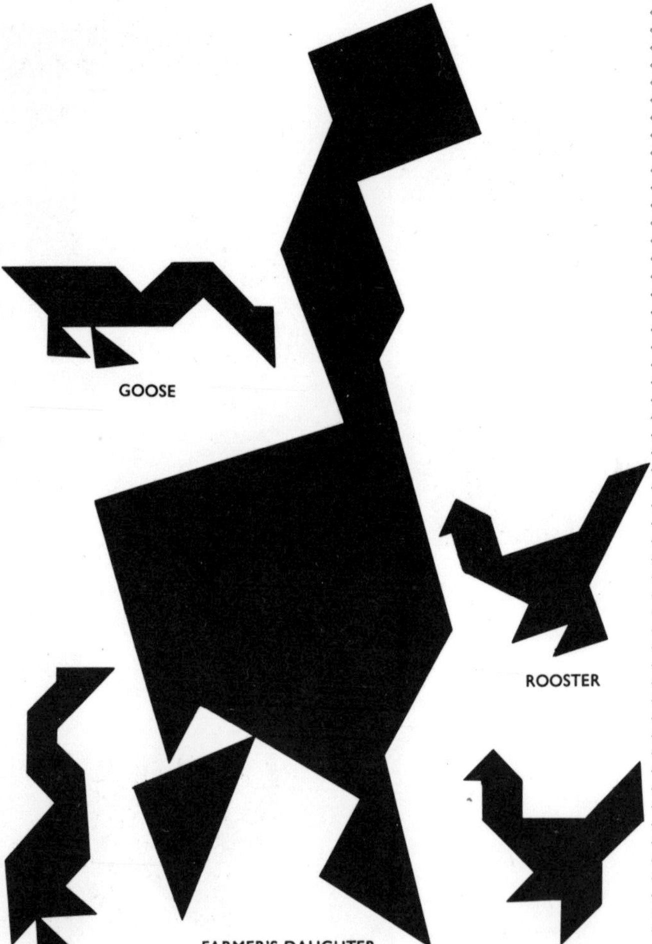

FARMER'S DAUGHTER

HEN

Pattern sizes: 2"; ⅝"

Solution on page 50

MARCO POLO VISITS KUBLAI KHAN'S COURT

THE KHAN

THRONE

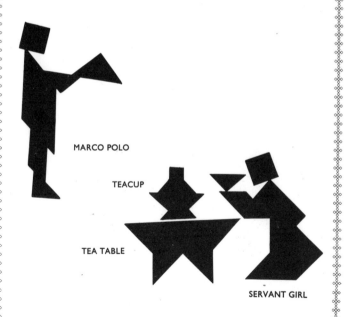

MARCO POLO

TEACUP

TEA TABLE

SERVANT GIRL

ONE

TWO

FIVE

THREE

FOUR

Pattern size: ¾"

Solution on page 52

SIX

SEVEN

ZERO

EIGHT

NINE

Pattern size: $\frac{3}{4}$"

Solution on page 53

Solution on page 54

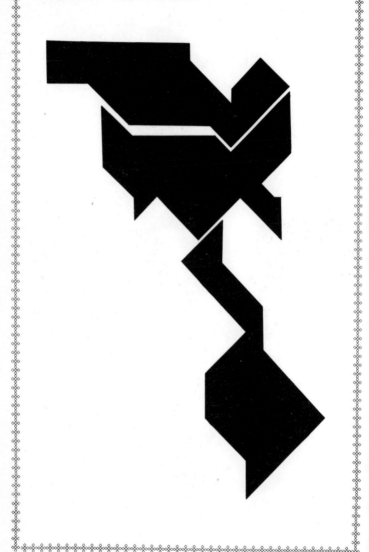

Pattern size: $1\frac{1}{4}''$

HOW ABOUT

MAKING

SOME TANGRAMS OF YOUR

VERY OWN!

Pattern size: $2\frac{1}{4}''$

Solution on page 55

PART TWO

TANGRAM-PATTERN SOLUTIONS

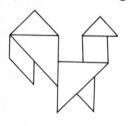

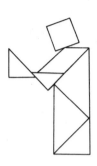

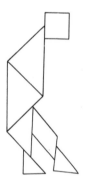

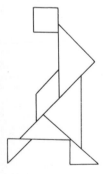

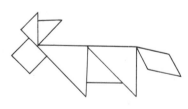

Solution for page 10

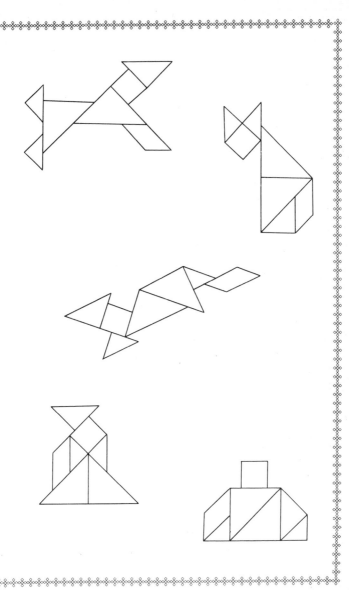

Solution for page 11

Solution for page 12

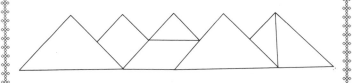

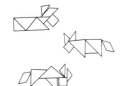

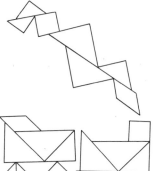

Solution for page 13

Solution for page 14

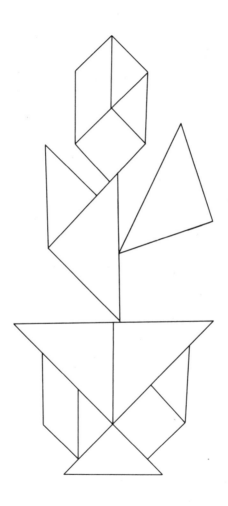

Solution for page 15

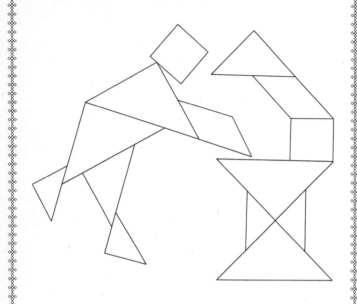

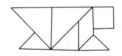

Solution for page 16

Solution for page 17

Solution for page 18

Solution for page 19

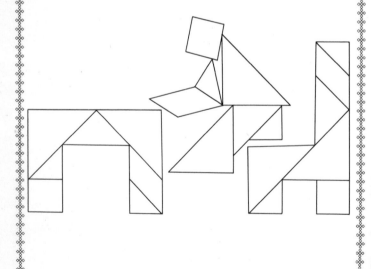

Solution for page 20

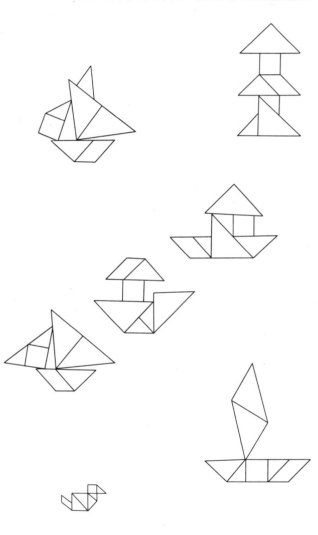

Solution for page 21

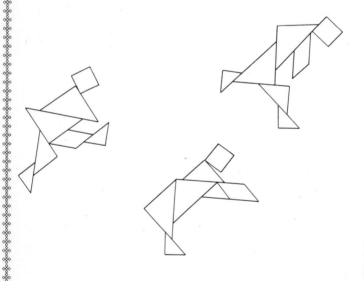

Solution for page 22

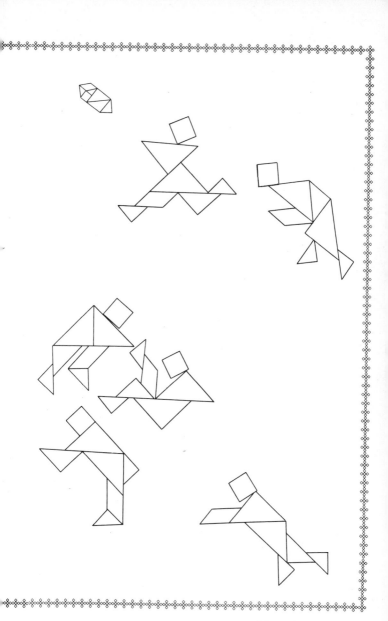

Solution for page 23

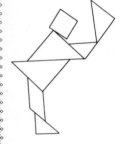

Solution for page 24

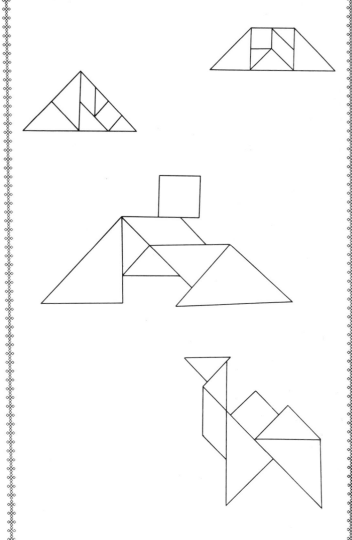

Solution for page 25

Solution for page 26

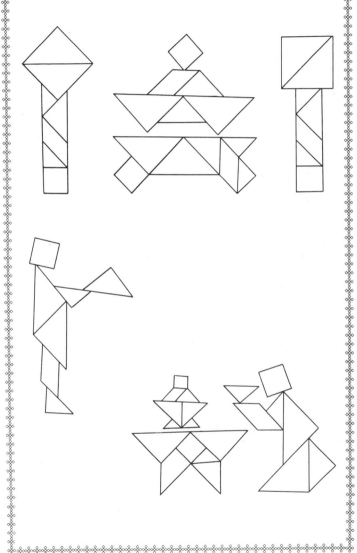

Solution for page 27

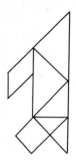

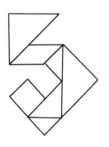

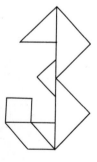

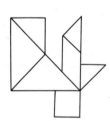

Solution for page 28

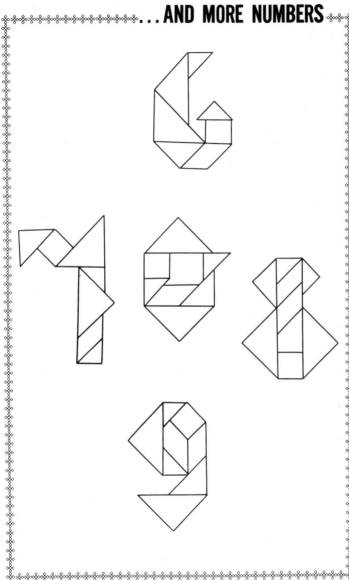

Solution for page 29

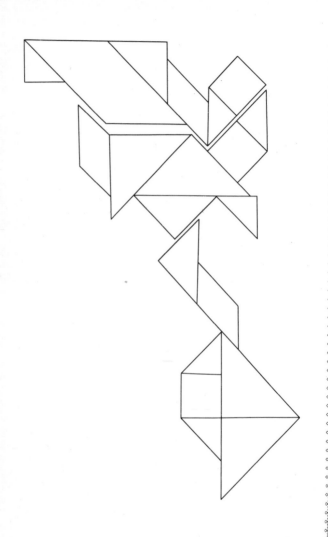

Solution for page 30

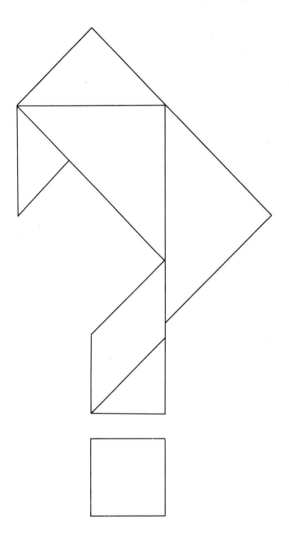

Solution for page 31

Other TUT BOOKS available:

**UNBEATEN TRACKS IN JAPAN: An Account of
Travels in the Interior Including Visits to the
Aborigines of Yezo and the Shrine of Nikko** *by
Isabella L. Bird*

ZILCH! The Marine Corps' Most Guarded Secret
by Roy Delgado

Please order from your bookstore or write directly
to:
CHARLES E. TUTTLE CO., INC.
Suido 1-chome, 2–6, Bunkyo-ku, Tokyo 112
or:
CHARLES E. TUTTLE CO., INC.
Rutland, Vermont 05701 U.S.A.